THE LAW
OF SUCCESS

T0160087

THE LAW
OF SUCCESS

by Napoleon Hill

The Original Classic

from the author of
Think and Grow Rich

Abridged and Introduced
by Mitch Horowitz

THE CONDENSED CLASSICS LIBRARY™

MEDIA

Published by Gildan Media LLC
aka G&D Media.
www.GandDmedia.com

The Law of Success was originally published in 1928
G&D Media Condensed Classics edition published 2018
Abridgement and Introduction copyright © 2015 by Mitch
Horowitz

FIRST EDITION: 2018

Cover design by David Rheinhardt of Pyrographx

Interior design by Meghan Day Healey of Story Horse, LLC.

ISBN: 978-1-7225-0052-8

Contents

The Science of Success

Y ou are about to experience Napoleon Hill's first comprehensive exploration of the principles of success. Hill began this project when, as a young journalist, he interviewed industrialist Andrew Carnegie in 1908. Carnegie urged the writer to make an intensive study of leaders across diverse fields to determine whether high achievers share a set of common traits.

Hill dedicated himself to this exploration for the next twenty years, and in 1928 he published his findings in a series of sixteen pamphlets called *The Law of Success*. This work became the basis for everything that followed in Hill's career, including his landmark *Think and Grow Rich* in 1937.

That later volume is primarily a digest and refinement of insights Hill first set down in *The Law of Success*. But some of Hill's most valuable ideas didn't make it into *Think and Grow Rich*. Hill's chapter here on "The

Golden Rule" is one of his clearest and most poignant statements on how your thoughts directly shape your experience. Likewise, his chapters on "Self-Control," "Accurate Thought," and "Concentration" highlight some of his sharpest insights.

The Law of Success remains Hill's most ambitious and wide-ranging exploration of the principles upon which greatness is built. This condensed edition retains all of the core points and strategies of Hill's original work.

While technology has obviously undergone radical changes since Hill published this book, his insights into human nature and the ingredients of achievement remain strikingly relevant.

If you are pursuing any personally meaningful aim—whether launching a business, attaining distinction as an artist or professional, or repairing injustice in the world—this book may prove one of the most significant learning experiences of your life. Return to it several times; memorize its lessons; and, above all, *use it.*

—Mitch Horowitz

The Master Mind

This is a course in the fundamentals of success.

Success is largely a matter of adapting to the changing circumstances of life in a spirit of harmony and poise. Harmony is based on understanding the forces around you. This course analyzes those forces and provides a blueprint to success.

To begin with, *you can never exercise power and attain success without the type of personality that influences others to willingly cooperate with you.* Each lesson teaches you how to build a winning personality through the fifteen laws of success. They are:

1. **A DEFINITE CHIEF AIM**
2. **SELF-CONFIDENCE**
3. **THE HABIT OF SAVING**
4. **INITIATIVE AND LEADERSHIP**
5. **IMAGINATION**

6. **ENTHUSIASM**

7. **SELF-CONTROL**

8. **THE HABIT OF DOING MORE THAN PAID FOR**

9. **PLEASING PERSONALITY**

10. **ACCURATE THOUGHT**

11. **CONCENTRATION**

12. **COOPERATION**

13. **PROFITING BY FAILURE**

14. **TOLERANCE**

15. **THE GOLDEN RULE**

The surest way to advance quickly through these principles, and into the fullness of your success, is with the aid of a Master Mind group. A Master Mind group consists of several people who coordinate their minds in pursuit of a goal.

The group may consist of any number from two or higher. Select the members of your Master Mind group carefully—the key ingredient is harmony and cooperation. You may focus on one group goal, or each member may have his own personal aims. Arrange a time to meet regularly to discuss your plans and ideas, and to exchange advice and guidance. When you're not together, hold each member's wishes and needs in your mind.

This friendly alliance, if carried out with purpose and harmony, will, in time, yield extraordinary results. For example, everyone in the group gains the ability to gather insight through the subconscious minds of all the other members. This produces a more vivid imaginative and mental state in which new ideas "flash" into your awareness.

Every high achiever I know has employed the power of the Master Mind. Do not neglect it.

A Definite Chief Aim

Probably ninety-five percent of all people drift aimlessly through life, without the slightest conception of the work for which they are best fitted, or even the need for a *definite* objective toward which to strive.

A person's acts are always in harmony with his dominating thoughts. Any *definite chief aim* that is deliberately fixed in the mind, with the determination to realize it, eventually saturates the subconscious until it influences all aspects of one's being.

Your *definite chief aim* should be selected with deliberate care. And after you select it you should write it out and place it where you will see it when you wake in the morning and retire at night. You must write down your aim—it is the first step towards its actualization.

You can impress your *definite chief aim* upon your subconscious through the principle called *autosuggestion*. In the simplest terms this is a suggestion that you make to yourself consistently and with deep feeling. Be certain that your *definite purpose* is constructive; that its attainment will bring hardship and misery to none; that it will bring you and your loved ones peace and prosperity; then apply the principle of self-suggestion, holding this idea constantly in your mind.

The subconscious is like a magnet, and when it has been vitalized and thoroughly saturated with any *definite purpose* it has a tendency to attract all that is necessary for the attainment of that purpose—in ideas, resources, circumstances, and people.

There is some *one thing* that you can do better than anyone else. Search until you find that particular line of endeavor, and make it your *definite chief aim*. Then direct all of your forces toward it with the belief that you are going to win. You will most likely attain the greatest success by finding what work you like best, for you generally succeed when you can thrown your whole heart and soul into something.

To be sure of success, your *definite chief aim* should be backed with a *burning desire* for its achievement. Merely desiring freedom would never release a man from prison if it were not sufficiently strong to cause him to do something to entitle himself to freedom.

You must experience your desire with a heartfelt passion. *Singleness of purpose* is essential for success.

Self-Confidence

You are now at one of the most unusual chapters in this book—because it consists largely of a *personal pledge*. I want you to consider this pledge very carefully, and then write it down and sign your name to it.

Repeat this pledge at least once a day until it has become a part of your mental makeup. Keep a copy of it before you as a daily remainder. By doing so you will again be making use of *autosuggestion*—or self-suggestion—to develop the crucial trait of self-confidence.

Never mind what anyone may say about your method. Outside your Master Mind group, you don't have to talk to anyone about it. In fact, it's probably best not to. Just remember that it is your business to succeed, and this creed, if mastered and applied, will take you a long way.

I believe in myself. I believe in my coworkers. I believe in my employer. I believe in my friends. I believe in my family. I believe that God will lend me everything I need to succeed if I do my best to earn it through faithful and honest service. I believe in prayer and will never close my eyes in sleep without praying for divine guidance to be patient with others and tolerant of those who do not believe as I do. I believe that success is the result of intellectual effort and does not depend upon blind luck or sharp-practices or double-crossing. I believe that I will get from life what I put into it, therefore I will conduct myself toward others as I would want them to act toward me. I will not spread or listen to slander and gossip. I will not slight my work no matter what I may see others doing. I will render the best service possible because I have pledged myself to succeed in life, and I know that true success is the result of conscientious and efficient effort. Finally, I will forgive those who offend me because I realize that I shall sometimes offend others and I will need their forgiveness.

Remember: Write this statement out, sign it, recite it daily, and keep it where you can see it.

The Habit of Saving

Saving money is a matter of habit. For this reason, we begin with a brief analysis of the *law of habit*.

The law of habit shapes your personality. Through repetition any act becomes a habit, and the mind may sometimes seem to be nothing more than a mass of motivating forces growing from our daily habits.

Here is how to develop the immensely valuable habit of saving:

FIRST

Through your *definite chief aim* set up in your mind an accurate and detailed description of what you want, including the amount of money you intend to earn. Your subconscious takes over this picture and uses it as a blueprint to mold your thoughts and actions into *practical plans*. Through the law of habit you keep the object of your *definite chief aim* fixed in your mind until it becomes firmly and permanently implanted there. This practice will erode the poverty consciousness and set up a prosperity consciousness. You will actually begin to DEMAND prosperity; you will begin to expect it; you will begin to prepare yourself to receive it and to use it wisely, thus paving the way for the *habit of saving*.

SECOND
Having in this manner increased your earning ability you make further use of the law of habit by committing, in the written statement of your *definite chief aim*, to save a fixed percentage of all that you earn. As your earnings increase, your savings increase in proportion, and you will be on the road to financial stability.

Initiative and Leadership

L
eadership is essential for attaining success—and *initiative* is the foundation upon which *leadership* sits.

Initiative is that exceedingly rare quality that impels a person to do what ought to be done *without being told to*. Leadership is found only among those who have acquired the *habit of initiative*.

Leadership is something you must invite yourself into; it will never thrust itself upon you. If you carefully analyze all the leaders with which you are familiar, you will see that they not only exercised *initiative*, but also went about their work with a *definite purpose*. You will further see that they possessed *self-confidence*. Anyone who lacks these traits is not really a leader.

Here is the exact procedure to become a person of *initiative* and *leadership*:

FIRST
You must eliminate all *procrastination*. This habit gnaws at the soul. Nothing is possible until you throw it off.

SECOND
You can best develop *initiative* by making it your business to interest those around you in doing the same. You learn best that which you teach.

THIRD
Understand that there are two kinds of *leadership*. One is as deadly as the other is helpful. The deadly brand belongs to pseudo-leaders who *force* their will on others. The brand we are after was seen in Abraham Lincoln: his leadership brought truth, justice, and understanding. Those qualities have engraved his name upon the heart of the world. Emulate them.

Imagination

You will never have a *definite purpose* in life, you will never have *self-confidence*, you will never have *initiative* and *leadership*, unless you first create these qualities in your *imagination* and see them as yours.

You may see how important *imagination* is when you stop to realize that it is the only thing in the world over which you have absolute control. Others may cheat you or deprive you of material wealth, but no one can deny you the control and use of your *imagination*.

Your imagination is the mirror of your soul, and you have every right to stand before that mirror and see yourself as you wish to be. You have *the right* to see in that mirror the mansion you intend to own, the business you plan to manage, the station in life you intend to occupy. *Your imagination belongs to you.* Use it! The more you use it the more efficiently it will serve you.

Your battle for achievement is already half won when *you know definitely what you want.*

The selection of your *definite chief aim* calls for both imagination and *decision.* The power of decision also grows with use. Prompt decision in compelling the *imagination* to create a *definite chief aim* gives you a more powerful capacity to reach decisions in other matters.

Enthusiasm

E nthusiasm is a state of mind that inspires you to *action*. But it does more—it is contagious, and it arouses everyone around you.

Enthusiasm is the vital force of life. The greatest leaders know how to instill enthusiasm in their followers. Enthusiasm is the most important factor in salesmanship. It is by far the most crucial factor in public speaking.

Mix enthusiasm with your work and it will seem neither hard nor monotonous. *Enthusiasm* will so energize your body that you can get along with less than half the usual amount of sleep and perform two to three times as much work as usual, without fatigue.

Enthusiasm is no mere figure of speech; it is a *vital force* through which you can recharge your body and develop a dynamic personality. Some are blessed with natural enthusiasm; others must acquire it. The procedure through which it may be developed is simple. It begins by doing the work that you like best. If you cannot, for the time being, engage in such work that is all more reason to adopt a *definite chief aim*, and you will begin to move toward it.

Lack of money and many other circumstances may force you to engage in work that you do not like. But no one can stop you from determining your *definite chief aim*; nor can anyone stop you from planning ways and means for translating that aim into reality; nor can anyone stop you from mixing *enthusiasm* with your plans.

When you are enthusiastic over your goods or services, or the speech you are delivering, your mental state becomes obvious to all who hear you. The tone with which you make a statement, more than the statement itself, carries conviction or fails to convince. Words are devitalized sounds unless colored with enthusiasm.

But take note: *Never express, through words or acts, something that does not harmonize with your beliefs—or you will lose the ability to influence others.*

I do not believe that I can afford to deceive anyone about anything; but *I know that I cannot afford to deceive myself.* To do so would destroy the power of my pen. It is only when I write with the *fire of enthusiasm* that my writing impresses others. *It is only when I speak from a heart that is bursting with belief in my message* that I can move my audience to accept it.

Self-Control

elf-control is the force through which you direct your enthusiasm to constructive ends. Without *self-control* enthusiasm resembles unharnessed lightening—it may strike a*nywhe*re, destroying life and property. The balanced person possesses both *enthusiasm* and *self-control*.

The majority of our griefs result from lack of self-control. Scripture is full of injunctions to *self-control*. It even urges us to love our enemies and to forgive those who injure us. The law of non-resistance runs like a golden cord throughout the Bible.

Where does *self-control* come from? Consider this very carefully: *Thought* is the only thing over which you have total dominion. This is of profound significance. It suggests that *thought* is your nearest approach to Divinity on this earthly plane. This fact carries another vital idea: namely, that *thought* is your most important tool; the one with which you may shape your destiny. Divine Providence did not make *thought* the sole power over which you have absolute control without associating that power with potentialities which, if understood and developed, would strain belief.

Self-control is solely a matter of thought-control.

You are searching for the magic key to power; and yet you have the key in your hands, and may use it the moment you learn to *control your thoughts.*

A student once asked how he could control his thoughts in a state of intense anger. I replied, *"In exactly the same way that you would change your manner and tone if you were in a heated argument with a family member and heard the doorbell ring, signaling that company was about to visit. You would control yourself because you would desire to."*

If you have ever faced a similar predicament, where you found it necessary to quickly conceal your feelings and change your facial expression, you know that it can be done *because you WANT TO!*

Back of all achievement, back of all *self-control*, back of all *thought control*, is that magic something called DESIRE! It is no exaggeration to say that you are limited only by the depth of your *desire*.

When your *desire* is strong enough you will appear to possess superhuman abilities. No one has ever explained this phenomenon of the mind, and perhaps no one ever will, but if you doubt that it exists you have only to experiment.

Don't say, "It can't be done," or that you are different from the thousands of people who have achieved noteworthy success. If you are "different" it is only because *they desired the object of their achievement with greater depth and intensity than you.*

The energy that most people dissipate through lack of self-control, or fritter away gossiping, would, if controlled and directed constructively, be sufficient to attain their *definite chief aim*, provided they have one.

The Habit of Doing More Than Paid For

Here is one of the most important laws of this philosophy: *A person is most efficient, and will more quickly and easily succeed, when engaged in work that he loves, or work that he performs for someone he loves.*

When the element of love enters any task, the quality of the work improves and the quantity increases. When engaged in work that you love it is no hardship to do more and better work than you are paid for; for this very reason you owe it to yourself to find the work you like best.

There are many reasons to do more than you are paid for, but two stand out:

FIRST

By establishing a reputation as someone who performs more and better work than paid for, you benefit by comparison with competitors who rarely show such commitment.

SECOND

Suppose that you want to develop a strong right arm. You could develop such an arm *only by giving it the hardest use*. Out of resistance comes strength. By performing more and better service than paid for, you not only develop your skill and ability but also can *command* greater remuneration than the majority who do not perform such service.

Try this experiment: For the next six months commit to rendering useful service to at least one person every day, for which *you neither expect nor accept monetary pay*. Go at this experiment with faith that it will prove to you one of the most powerful laws of success: that you succeed best and quickest by helping others to succeed.

Pleasing Personality

Your personality is the sum total of your characteristics and appearance. The clothes you wear, the lines in your face, the vitality of your body, your handshake, your tone of voice, the thoughts you think, the character you have developed by those thoughts—all are parts of your *personality*.

Whether your personality is attractive is another matter.

By far the most important part of your personality is your *character*, and is therefore the part that is not visible. The style of your clothes and their appropriateness also constitute an important part of your personality, for it is true that people derive first impressions from your outward appearance.

There is one way to express your personality that will *always attract*: *taking a heartfelt interest in others*.

Study people closely enough to find something about them or their work that you *truly* admire. Talk to them about it. Show genuine interest in it. Only in this way can you develop a personality that will be irresistibly *attractive.*

Cheap flattery has the opposite effect. It repels instead of attracting. It is so shallow that even the ignorant easily detect it.

As noted, *character* is the most important factor in *personality*. How can you build *character*? Follow these steps:

FIRST
Identify people whose characters have the qualities you wish to emulate, and develop these qualities through *autosuggestion.*

SECOND
Let the dominating thought of your mind be a picture of the person that you are *deliberately building.*

THIRD
Find at least one person each day, and more if possible, in whom you see some good quality and *praise it*. But remember, this praise must be *genuine* and not insincere flattery.

I cannot over-emphasize the benefits of praising, openly and enthusiastically, the good qualities in others; for this habit will soon reward you with a feeling of self-respect and manifestation of gratitude from others, which will modify your entire personality.

Accurate Thought

Y ou cannot succeed without *accurate thought*. *Accurate thought* involves two fundamentals. First, you must separate *facts* from mere *information*. Much "information" is not based upon facts. Second, you must divide *facts* into two classes: *important* and *unimportant*.

All facts that *aid* your pursuit of your *definite chief aim* (without violating the rights of others) are *important* and *relevant*. All that you cannot use are the opposite. If you direct your attention exclusively to the *important facts*—those that contribute to the realization of your aim—you will attain a special clarity.

You must also avoid the vulgar and self-destructive habit of spreading and listening to gossip. If you permit yourself to be swayed by all manner of information—especially rumors and gossip—you will never become an *accurate thinker*, and you will not attain your *definite chief aim*.

We will now explore a special form of *thought* that does much more than gather and organize facts. In many ways, this form of thought is the keynote of this course. We will call it *creative thought*. With a few exceptions man has not yet recognized *creative thought* as the connecting link to the power of *infinite intelligence*.

To understand how this occurs we return to the topic of *autosuggestion*. The sense impressions arising from your environment, or from the statements and actions of others, are mere ordinary suggestions; but the sense impressions that *you place in your own mind*—that you deliberately and confidently dwell upon, think of at every opportunity, and mentally picture and *feel*—are the product of self-suggestion, or *autosuggestion*.

Autosuggestion is the telegraph line over which you register in your subconscious the aim you wish to *create* in physical form.

The subconscious is the intermediary between the conscious *thinking mind* and *infinite intelligence*. You can invoke the aid of *infinite intelligence* through the *subconscious* only by giving it clear instructions as to what you want. Hence the critical need for a *definite chief aim*.

The subconscious records the suggestions that you send it through autosuggestion, and invokes the aid of infinite intelligence in translating these suggestions into their natural physical form, through natural means which are in no way out of the ordinary.

First, you must select the picture to be recorded (your *definite chief aim*). Then you fix your conscious mind upon this purpose with such intensity that it communicates with the subconscious through autosuggestion, and registers that picture. You then watch for and expect manifestations of the physical realization of that picture.

Bear in mind that you do not sit down and wait, nor go to sleep, with the expectation that *infinite intelligence* has granted your desire. No, you go right ahead doing your daily work *with full faith and confidence that natural ways and means for the attainment of your definite purpose will open to you at the proper time and in a suitable manner.*

Infinite intelligence will not build you a home and deliver it ready to enter. But *infinite intelligence* will open the way and provide the necessary means, including insights, intuitions, and ideas, which allow you to build your own house. Do not reply upon miracles for your *definite chief aim*; rely upon the power of *infinite intelligence* to guide you, through natural channels and laws, to its attainment.

Concentration

To move safely and accurately toward a target you must *concentrate* on it. Two important laws enter into the act of *concentrating* on a given desire. One is the law of autosuggestion, which we have already reviewed; the other is the law of habit, which we will now consider in further detail.

Habit grows from environment and repetition—from doing and thinking the same thing over and over. Except for rare occasions when the mind rises above environment, we draw the material out of which *thought* is created from our surroundings, and *habit* crystalizes this thought into a permanent fixture.

To attain success, you must develop habits that lead toward constructive thoughts and actions in the direction of your *definite chief aim*. Follow this procedure to acquire the habits you need:

FIRST

At the beginning of the formation of a new habit put force and enthusiasm into your expression. *Feel what you think.* Remember that you are taking the first steps toward making a new mental path; it is much harder at first than it will be later. Make the path as clear and as deep as you can at the beginning, so that you can readily see it the next time you wish to follow it.

SECOND

Keep your attention firmly *concentrated* on the new path you are building, and keep you mind far away from the old paths.

THIRD

Travel over your newly made paths as often as possible. Make opportunities for doing so. The more you traverse these new paths the sooner they will become familiar and easily travelled.

FOURTH

Resist the temptation to travel over the older, easier paths that you have used in the past. Every time you resist a temptation, you grow stronger.

FIFTH

Be sure that you have mapped out the right path as your *definite chief aim*—and then charge at it without fear or doubt.

Cooperation

Success cannot be attained singlehandedly. It requires *cooperative effort*. Even a hermit in the wilderness is *dependent* upon forces outside himself for existence. The more he becomes a part of civilization, the more he *depends* upon *cooperative effort*.

If your philosophy is based upon cooperation instead of competition you will not only acquire the necessities and luxuries of life with less effort, but you will enjoy an additional reward in *happiness*. Fortunes acquired through cooperative effort inflict no scars upon the hearts of their owners.

Ordinary cooperative effort produces power. But cooperative effort that is based upon complete harmony of purpose develops *superpower*. Gave a person of average ability a sufficiently visualized and passionately felt motive and he will develop superpower. Men work harder for *an ideal* than they will for money. Remember this when searching for a motive to develop group cooperation.

Men generally respond to three major motivating forces:

1. The motive of self-preservation.
2. The motive of sexual contact.
3. The motive of financial and social power.

Regardless of who you are, or your *definite chief aim*, if you depend upon others—as almost all of us do—you must present them with a motive strong enough to ensure their full cooperation.

Profiting by Failure

What we typically call *failure* is, in reality, *temporary defeat*. Moreover, this temporary defeat often proves a blessing, for it jolts us and redirects our energies along different and more desirable paths.

Sound character is usually the outcome of reverses, setbacks, and temporary defeat.

Neither temporary defeat nor adversity spell failure to one who looks upon such things as a teacher. A great and lasting lesson appears in every reverse and defeat— and, usually, it could be learned in no other way.

Ralph Waldo Emerson explored this principle in his great essay "Compensation." If you haven't read it, do so—and reread it every three months.

I used to *hate* my enemies. But this was before I learned how well they were serving me by keeping me everlastingly on the alert, lest some weak spot in my character provide an opening through which I might be damaged. Enemies discover your defects and point them out; friends, even if they see them, say nothing.

I am convinced that failure is Nature's plan through which she hurdle-jumps men of destiny and prepares them to do their work. Failure is Nature's great crucible in which she burns the dross from the human heart and purifies the metal of a man so that it can stand the test of hard usage.

Tolerance

Always remember these two facts about *intolerance*.

FIRST

Intolerance makes enemies; it disintegrates the organized forces of society; it dethrones reason and substitutes mob psychology in its place. *Intolerance* is a form of ignorance that must be mastered before enduring success may be attained.

SECOND

Intolerance is the chief disintegrating force in the organized religions of the world, where it plays havoc with the greatest power for good on earth by breaking it up into small sects, which spend as much time opposing each other as in combating evil.

Anything that impedes the progress of civilization also stands as a barrier to each individual.

I once encountered intolerance in myself, and I vowed to *unlearn much that I had previously considered the truth.* I discovered that I had acquired my views of religion, politics, economics, and many other important subjects simply by "picking up" what my family believed.

Most of my views were unsupported by even a reasonable hypothesis, much less facts. Imagine suddenly discovering that most of your philosophy had been built on bias and prejudice.

I urge you to learn how and where you acquired your philosophy of life in order to trace your prejudices and biases to their original source—and to discover, as I did, the degree to which you are the result of training you received before the age of fifteen.

The Golden Rule

For more than twenty-five years I have been observing how men behave in positions of power, and I have seen that the man who attains power in any way other than a slow, step-by-step process is in constant danger of destroying himself and all whom he influences.

For more than four thousand years humanity has preached the Golden Rule as the foundation of good conduct. But the world has accepted the letter while totally missing the spirit of this universal injunction. We acknowledge the Golden Rule merely as a sound principle—but we have failed to understand the *inner law* upon which it is based.

The Golden Rule means to do unto others as you would wish them to do unto you. But why? What is the *real* reason for this kindly consideration of others?

The reason is this: There is an eternal law by which we reap what we sow. When you select the rule of conduct by which to guide your life, you are more likely be fair and just if you *know* that you are setting into motion a *power* that will run its course in the lives of others, returning, finally, to help or hinder you, according to its nature.

It is your choice to deal unjustly with others, but if you understand the law upon which the Golden Rule is based, you must know that your unjust deals will return to you.

You cannot pervert or change the course of this law—*but you can adapt yourself to its nature and thereby use it as an irresistible power that will carry you to heights of achievement.*

This law does not stop merely by flinging back at you your *acts* of injustice and unkindness; it goes further—much further—and *returns to you the results of every thought that you release.*

Therefore, it is advisable not only to "do unto others as you wish them to do unto you." But to make full use of this great Universal Law you must "*think of others as you wish them to think of you.*" The law upon which the Golden Rule is based begins affecting you, for good or evil, the moment you release a *thought.*

Understand this law and you understand *all* that the Bible has to reveal. The Bible presents one unbroken chain of evidence that man is the maker of his own destiny.

All your *acts* toward others, and even your *thoughts* of others, are registered in your subconscious through the principle of autosuggestion, thereby building your own character in exact duplicate. Can you see how important it is to guard those acts and thoughts?

You cannot act toward another without having first created the nature of that act in your own *thought, and you cannot release a thought without planting the sum and substance of it in your own subconscious, there to become a part of your character.*

Grasp this simple principle and you will understand why you cannot afford to hate or envy another person. You will also understand why you cannot afford to strike back at those who do you an injustice. Likewise, you will understand the injunction, "Return good for evil."

Throughout this course I have emphasized one particular principle for the purpose of revealing that your personality is the sum total of your *thoughts* and *acts*—and that you come to resemble the nature of your dominating *thoughts*.

Man, alone, has the power to transform his *thoughts* into physical reality. Use the palace of your mind methodically, carefully, and deliberately—and you will reconstruct on the outside those dreams that dwell within.

About the Authors

NAPOLEON HILL was born in 1883 in Wise County, Virginia. He was employed as a secretary, a reporter, the manager of a coalmine and a lumberyard, and attended law school, before he began working as a journalist for *Bob Taylor's Magazine,* an inspirational and general-interest journal. In 1908 the job led to his interviewing steel magnate Andrew Carnegie. The encounter changed the course of Hill's life. Carnegie believed success could be distilled into definite principles that anyone could follow. He urged Hill to interview the greatest industrialists, financiers, and inventors of the era to discover these principles. Hill pursued the challenge for twenty years, resulting in his landmark volume *The Law of Success* in 1928. The sixteen-volume work formed the basis for Hill's worldwide sensation *Think and Grow Rich* in 1937. Hill dedicated the rest of his life to documenting and refining the principles of success. The motivational pioneer died in 1970 in South Carolina.

MITCH HOROWITZ, who abridged and introduced this volume, is the PEN Award-winning author of books including *Occult America* and *The Miracle Club: How*

Thoughts Become Reality. The Washington Post says Mitch "treats esoteric ideas and movements with an even-handed intellectual studiousness that is too often lost in today's raised-voice discussions." Follow him @MitchHorowitz.